Mel Bay Presents

Graded Repertoire for Guitar

Book One

Stanley Yates Series

D1283286

A compact disc (99630CD) of the music in this book is now available. The publisher strongly recommends the use of these recordings along with the text to insure accuracy of interpretation and ease in learning.

At the authors request pages 2, 4, 10, 12, 28, 54, 92 and 96 are left blank.

MEL BAY ®

Visit us on the Web at www.melbay.com — E-mail us at email@melbay.com

Contents by Composer (1) easy; (2) moderate; (3) challenging

Foreword

If one of the most attractive qualities of the guitar is the diversity of its repertoire, then one of the most rewarding aspects of guitar study is also one of its challenges — the guitar student deals not only with historical musical styles that span a period of nearly five-hundred years, but with a wide range of contemporary musical styles as well. Balancing the challenges with the rewards, while maintaining steady technical and musical progress, is surely the fundamental requirement for productive and pleasurable study of the instrument.

This new series of graded repertoire for guitar has been put together with the aim of providing students with the most attractive, stylistically comprehensive, and inspiring music available, while at the same time realistically meeting the pedagogical needs of their teachers. Students and teachers will therefore find in these volumes some of the most representative and attractive music of the major repertoire areas of the instrument, both historical and contemporary, carefully selected, graded and edited for pedagogical appropriateness. While some of this music is very well known, much of it is not to be found in similar collections.

Although this first volume is not intended for the *complete* beginner, with a little experience students should soon be able to supplement the material provided in their method books with repertoire taken from this book.

Within the overall introductory nature of this first volume, the pieces are grouped according to three levels (determined by technical and/or musical factors). Within each level, pieces are further grouped (when possible) in the following unmarked categories:

- classical (nineteenth-century) music
- early and traditional/folk music (except level 1)
- contemporary music

This organization should help students, as they progress, not only to maintain a balanced-diet of musical styles and genres, but also to pick-and-choose pieces appropriate to their needs from within the overall level. It is also possible to work through this book from cover-to-cover, experiencing a constant variety of musical styles and techniques within the overall progressive order of the material.

No collection of pieces, no matter how carefully organized and edited, can substitute for the systematic approach of an instrumental method book. It is therefore expected that this volume will be used in conjunction with a method book, preferably with the guidance of a teacher. For self-teachers, I have included brief study notes, where appropriate.

A Few Technical Issues

Right-Hand Fingering

Most of the pieces in this book include fingering suggestions for the right hand. At first sight, it might be difficult to recognize the patterns underlying these fingerings, and the temptation may be to ignore them! This would be a missed opportunity to develop the good habits that derive from using systematic right-hand fingerings. One of the most important goals of early right-hand training is the acquisition of *automatic fingering* - the ability, based on the repeated use of systematic fingerings, to play standard patterns and textures automatically. Of course, many players continue to write fingerings into their score long after these systems have been assimilated, and most pieces contain passages that require some thought to determine appropriate fin-

gerings. In either case, to help the process of under standing and developing automatic fingering for the right-hand, and since few method books discuss the issue, a simple outline of the systems used in this book may be helpful.

There are only two fundamental fingering systems for the right hand, though the majority of musical textures move constantly back and forth between them. The first, used for chords and arpeggio textures, assigns each of the fingers to its own string:

The second, used for scales, alternates between two fingers (usually *i-m* or *m-i*) on the same string:

In both arpeggio and scale/melodic textures, the aim is to avoid repeating the same finger from note to note (repeating a finger not only reduces speed and facility but also inhibits the ability to produce a good sound on any but the slowest notes of a passage).

With single-string alternation technique (sequences of *i-m* or *m-i*) it is important to arrange the sequence of right-hand fingers so that moving from one string to another is made as efficiently as possible. While it is possible to use an occasional awkward string-crossing, especially on adjacent strings, a series of awkward crossings can be quite confusing. The interjection of the *a* finger in a sequence of *i-m* or *m-i* alternation is the easiest way to avoid an awkward string crossing:

Since, for most players, the independence between the middle and ring fingers is usually considerably less than between any other pair of fingers, *a-m* alternation beyond two notes is generally avoided, except as an exercise.

However, there are always exceptions (and individual ways of doing things)!

Left-Hand Slurs

Simple ascending and descending slurs are introduced in Level 2 of this book, more advanced ones in Level 3. The success of an ascending slur is determined almost entirely by hand position (not by force). To determine the correct hand position for an ascending slur, when practicing: put the finger on the second note of the slur, raise it, play the slur. Descending slurs take only a little more work: place the finger on first note of the slur, with normal pressure; pluck the first note of the slur with a right-hand finger; *pluck* the second note of the slur with the slurring finger (of the left-hand).

Barres

A few pieces in this book employ a brief two or three-string barre. Take care to cover only the number of strings indicated, not more. If you have trouble holding down a barre, try pointing your index finger — barre technique really is something that develops through the act of trying, as the muscles and joints of the finger become oriented to something they otherwise have little use for in day-to-day life (unlike the scratching and gripping-type actions used for most other facets of playing the guitar).

Damping

Careful attention should be paid to damping (silencing) unwanted sounds, especially in the bass. Three common situations (often ignored by students!) that require damping with the right-hand thumb are: (1) to prevent an open bass-string from continuing to ring beyond its written value (usually, the thumb returns to damp the note immediately *after* playing the next bass note): (2) to silence a bass-note that is followed by a rest (the thumb plays and damps); (3) in playing staccato notes (again, the thumb plays and damps). Of course, the fingers use these techniques from time to time as well.

Practicing

A few suggestions that might help make your practice more productive:

- Don't practice at tempos faster than you can think about what you are trying to do (seems obvious!)
- Concentrate on one aspect of the piece at a time (right hand, left hand, dynamics, sound, etc.)
- Isolate difficult spots and practice them separately (and slowly)
- Don't repeat the same mistakes over and over - you'll learn them!
- Practice away from the guitar, looking at the score, and in your imagination

Practicing Arpeggio Studies

In most guitar methods arpeggio studies are among the first pieces a student will study, since they help establish automatic alternation of the right-hand fingers, as well as orienting the left-hand to common dispositions on the fingerboard (they sound good too!). With this in mind, it is always a good idea to practice the right-hand pattern separately (using open strings or using a single chord). It is also a good idea to play through the chord progression as a series of block chords, noting the connections between each successive pair of chords and the hand positions involved. However, it is not usually a good idea to actually play an arpeggio study by placing each new chord as a full "chord shape." Instead, the left-hand fingers should be placed sequentially, as the arpeggio pattern progresses. This ensures smooth chord changes, helps establish good habits for the left hand, and makes pieces a whole lot easier to play! A "slow-motion" description of how this works:

On the first note of each new chord (usually the first beat of the measure), as the thumb plays:

- lift all fingers not required for the next chord (leave any common fingers pressed down)
- place at least the finger needed for the first note of the new chord (if necessary) and the next finger as well (*unless* that finger plays the last note of the previous chord)
- add any remaining fingers as you need them

For example,

This sequential technique for the left hand is essential for accuracy and smoothness (legato) and can be used, in almost any guitar piece.

Dynamic Markings

Pay attention to the written dynamics and other expression markings! These markings are so essential to musical expression that, in this first volume, I have silently added them to many of the pieces that contained none (or few) in the original versions. In addition, written expression marks are only a starting point — individual players should augment them according to their own musical feeling.

Metronome markings

Metronome markings are provided for all of the pieces in this volume, but should be regarded as general guides only.

Stanley Yates
August, 2001

The Composers

Dionisio AGUADO (1784-1849)
A Spanish guitarist who associated closely with his fellow Spanish guitarist Fernando Sor in Paris. Aguado is best known today for his guitar method, the most detailed account of guitar technique of the time.

Matteo CARCASSI (1792-1853)
An Italian guitarist who worked mainly in Paris, one of the second wave of Italian guitarists to move there. His style is a little more romantic than that of Carulli, whose career was eclipsed by Carcassi. Both his guitar method, op. 16 and his 25 studies, op. 60 have remained in use to the present day.

Turlough CAROLAN (1670-1738)
A blind Irish harp player who made his living travelling from house to house, composing tunes for his prospective hosts on the way. He was the last great figure in the Irish harp tradition, and his surviving melodies were written down and published by his son, soon after his death. His surname is often (incorrectly) given as "O'Carolan."

Ferdinando CARULLI (1770-1841)
An Italian guitarist who spent most of his career in Paris, being perhaps the principal guitarist of the city before the arrival of Sor and, later, his fellow Italian Carcassi. He was the most prolific guitar composer of the time (probably of any time!), his works reaching well over 300 opus numbers, many of which contained dozens of individual pieces.

Carlo DOMENICONI
An Italian guitarist and composer who spent many years living and working in Turkey. One of his guitar works, *Koyunbaba*, based on Turkish music, is among the most-performed concert works of the present time.

Mauro GIULIANI (1780-1829)
An Italian guitarist who worked mainly in Vienna, where he was among the most celebrated instrumental performers of the time. He was personally associated with such illustrious musical figures as Beethoven, Rossini and Paganini, and took part in the first performance of Beethoven's Seventh Symphony (probably as a cellist).

Roger HUDSON
An American composer and guitarist whose music combines classical and popular influences.

Nikita KOSHKIN
A Russian guitarist and composer whose music has been performed and recorded by many leading performers, including himself. His best-known pieces include *The Prince's Toys* and the *Usher Waltz*.

Antonio Jimenez MANJON (1866-1919)
A Spanish guitarist and composer who worked mainly in Argentina. Although blind from childhood, he apparently left Spain for Paris, alone, at the age of 14.

Guillame MORLAYE (c1515-c1565)
A French guitarist and lutenist who lived in Paris, where he received a Royal privilege that allowed him to print and publish music for lute and guitar.

Antonio NAVA (1775-1828)
An Italian guitarist who worked mainly in Milan. Though virtually none of his music is available today, his guitar method was one of the most successful Italian guitar publications of its time.

Jean Phillip RAMEAU (1683-1764)
An important French harpsichordist, composer and music theorist.

Stepan RAK
An innovative Czech guitarist and composer, whose music often draws upon visual imagery. Among his best-known pieces are *Elegy*, *Czech Fairy Tales* and *Voces de Profundis* — a piece inspired by the Alfred Hitchcock movie *Psycho*.

Lucas de RIBAYEZ (fl. 1680-1700)
A Spanish guitarist about whom little is known beyond his book of guitar music, *Luz y norte musicale* (most of which was taken from an earlier book by Gaspar Sanz).

Ernest SHAND (1868-1924)
An English guitarist, famous during his lifetime as an actor. A collection of his guitar works, otherwise out of print for almost a hundred years, has recently been republished by Mel Bay Publications in the Stanley Yates Series.

Fernando SOR (1778-1839)
A Spanish guitarist and composer who worked mainly in Paris and London. Widely regarded as the finest guitar composer of his time, he also composed orchestral music, opera, and ballet. In addition to several extended concert works, he is well-known to guitarists today for his sets of attractive studies.

Milan TESAR
A Czech guitarist and composer who has written several collections of pieces that combine classical guitar technique with popular musical idioms.

Andrew WINNER
An American guitarist and composer who has specialized in repertoire for younger students.

Stanley YATES
That would be me — see the back cover!

Andrew YORK
An American guitarist and composer whose music has been recorded by many leading performers, including himself.

Jaime Mirtenbaum ZENAMON
A Brazilian guitarist and composer whose numerous works include several sets of character pieces for students.

Terminology

The following terms and symbols are used in this book.

<u>Fingering and guitar symbols</u>

1, 2, 3, 4 — fingers of the left (fretting) hand, index, middle, ring and little, respectively

(2) — alternative left-hand fingering

i, m, a, p — fingers of the right (plucking) hand, index, middle, ring and thumb, respectively

Circled numbers indicate strings

II³ — barre (in this case at the second fret covering the first 3 strings)

- indicates that a finger remains on the same string, either at the same fret or at a new one

left-hand slur

 optional slur or editorial slur (not present in the original source)

 brings attention to a finger movement

 "roll," arpeggiate the chord (from the lowest note to the highest)

 harmonics

har.	(natural) harmonic
art. har.	artificial harmonic
vib.	vibrato, pull the string back and forth
l.v.	*lasciare vibrare* - let the notes ring over one another
tamboro	percussion, banging on the guitar
rasg.	*rasgueado*, strumming
pont.	*ponticello*, pluck near the bridge
dolce	sweet, pluck near the fingerboard

<u>Musical terminology</u>

"In 1"	in one beat per measure
Largo	slow
Adagio	slow
Lento	slow
Andante	walking pace - between slow and moderate
Andantino	on the slow side of moderate
Moderato	a normal, comfortable tempo
Allegretto	on the lively side of moderato
Allegro	lively, fast
Vivo	lively, fast
Tempo ad lib	you choose the tempo
a tempo	return to the former tempo
rit.	slower
pp	*pianissimo*, very soft
p	*piano*, soft
mp	*mezzo piano*, a little bit soft
mf	*mezzo forte*, a bit loud, normal volume
f	*forte*, loud
ff	*fortissimo*, very loud
sf or *fz*	play this one note louder than the surrounding ones
cresc.	*crescendo*, get progressively louder
dim.	*diminuendo*, get progressively softer
poco	a little bit
molto	a lot
più	more

sempre	always
sim.	*simile*, the same
lunga	long, a long time
grazioso	gracefully
smorzando	dying away
mysterioso	mysteriously
D.C.	*da capo* - go back to the beginning
Fine	finish, the end
Coda	the ending section of a piece
𝄐	fermata, pause as long as you like
,	short pause, breath
<	like *crescendo*, getting louder
>	like *diminuendo*, getting softer

<u>Articulation symbols</u>

accent, play this note louder

staccato, this note should not sound for its full written duration

tenuto, this note sounds for its full value (and a little bit more)

Level 1

2 Preludes

No. 1 in a-minor

i-m / i-a

From *En Mode - 22 Easy Character Pieces for Guitar*.
© 2001 Mel Bay Publications. Used with permission.

No. 2 in C

i-m-i / i-a-i

Moderate tempo [♩ = c.116]

Malagueña (Spanish Dance)

Moderately fast (in 1) [♩. = c.72]

Arranged by Stanley Yates

Matteo CARCASSI
(1792-1853)

3 Arpeggio Studies (from op. 59)

RH: a-m
LH: free-finger / fixed-finger changes

No. 1 in E

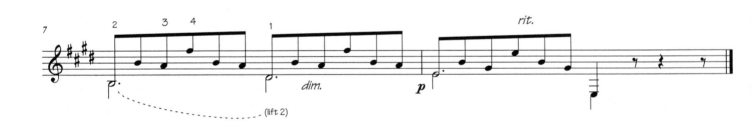

From *Méthode complète pour la guitare, op. 59* (Paris, c. 1840).

16

No. 2 in A

LH: free and fixed-finger changes

No. 3 in e-minor

Ferdinando CARULLI
(1770-1841)

[Level 1]

Study in a-minor (from op. 27)

p-i-m
LH: free and fixed-finger changes

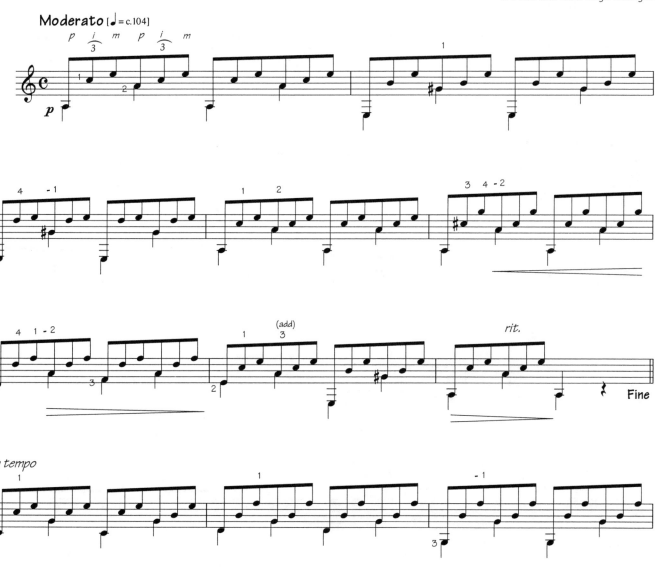

D. C al Fine

From *Méthode complète pour guitare, op. 27* (Paris, c. 1811).

Ferdinando CARULLI
(1770-1841)

[Level 1]

Waltz in C (op. 241, no.1)

im & ma chords / i-m alternation

mm14-15. The first finger must jump from the second string to the first;
try to avoid clipping the C by moving to the first string only as the right-
hand finger plucks the new note (practice this part separately).

From *Methode complète pour pincer le guitare, op. 241* (Paris, c. 1825).

Ferdinando CARULLI
(1770-1841)

Waltz in G (op. 241, no.4)

RH: m-i & a-i /
im chords

From *Methode complète pour pincer le guitare, op. 241* (Paris, c. 1825).

Fernando SOR
(1778-1839)

Andante in C, op. 35 no. 1

arpeggio / alternation mixture

From *Vingt Quatre Exercises, op. 35* (Paris, c. 1828).

Ernest SHAND
(1868-1924)

[Level 1]

Study in E (from op. 100)

LH: guide-finger position change

From *Improved Method for Guitar, op. 100* (London, 1896).

23

Stanley YATES

Folksong

i-m alternation /
damping & articlualtion

This piece can also be practiced using a strict pattern of
right-hand finger alternation throughout, i-m or m-i.

From *En Mode - 22 Easy Character Pieces for Guitar*.
© 2001 Mel Bay Publications. Used with permission.

Farewell Summer

Andante (in 2) [♩ = c.72]

3-part texture

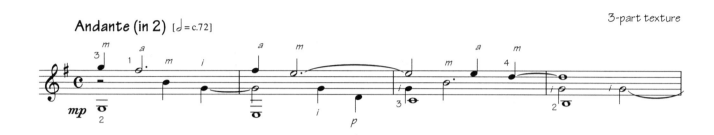

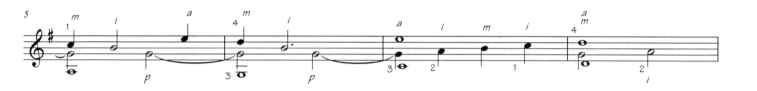

This piece uses a three-voice texture: an upper melody, a bass part (in long notes) and an inner voice part (which sometimes answers the upper voice). Try to distinguish the parts by using a fuller sound for the upper voice and bass and a clearer sound for the inner voice.

Soñando - "Dreaming" (no. 3 from 20 *Epigrammes*)

p-i-m-a
syncopation

In measures 1-9 hold the fingers close to their target frets before placing.
Practice the rhythm, before playing, by counting "1 & 2 & 3 & 4 &," gradually
replacing the "3" with a whisper.

Level 2

Ferdinando CARULLI
(1770-1841)

3 Preludes (from op. 114)

No. 1 in C

LH: "sequential" chord changes

[Moderato] [♩= c.116]

From *Vingt-quatre preludes pour la guitare, op. 114* (Paris, c. 1816)

No. 2 in D

LH: weaker fingers / preparation

To help make smooth chord changes, some of the chords in this piece
are played with the weaker left-hand fingers. Practice the chords as isolated
block chords to get used to the fingerings. In measures 8 and 11 be sure to
prepare the indicated fingers as close to their target frets as is comfortable
at the points marked.

No. 3 in G

[Moderato] [♩ = c.100]

31

Ferdinando CARULLI
(1770-1841)

Waltz in G (op. 121, no.2)

LH: fixed-finger / cross-string reach

From *Vingt-Quatre Pièces pour Guitarre op. 121* (Paris, c. 1815).

Ferdinando CARULLI
(1770-1841)

Contredance in C (op. 121, no. 10)

RH: m-i & a-i alternation / pim chords
LH: brief i² barre

From *Vingt-quatre pièces pour guitare seule, op. 121* (Paris, c. 1816)

Ferdinando CARULLI
(1770-1841)

Andante in a-minor (from op. 27)

LH: simple ascending slurs / full first position
RH: damping

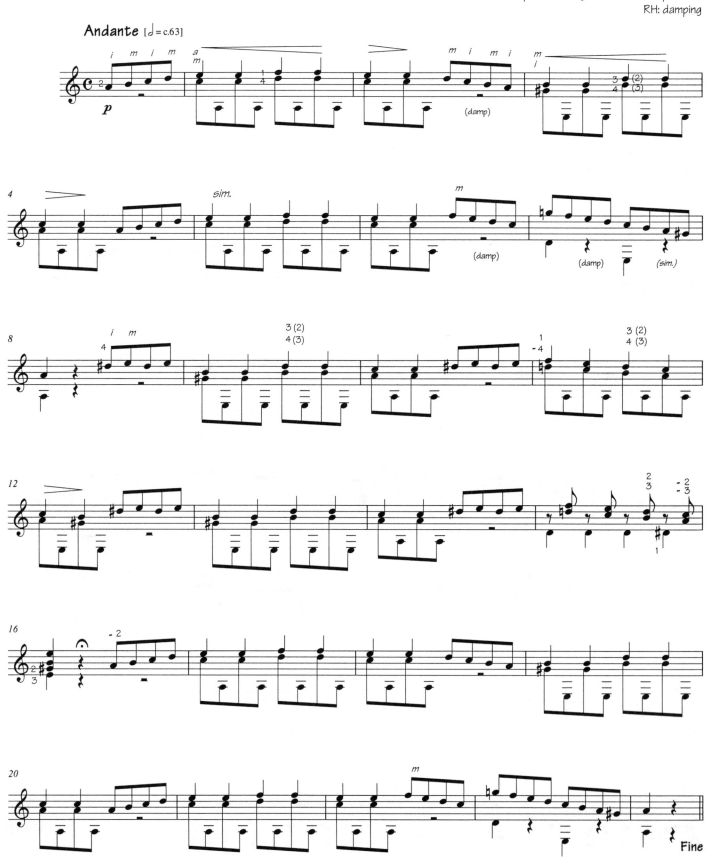

From *Méthode complète pour la guitare, op. 27* (Paris, c. 1811).

34

D. C. al Fine

35

Ferdinando CARULLI

(1770-1841)

Andante in G (op. 241, no.5)

Engraving of Carulli from his
Guitar Method (Paris, c1811).

Ferdinando Carulli

From *Methode complète pour pincer le guitare, op. 241* (Paris, c. 1825).

Mateo CARCASSI
(1792-1853)

Andantino grazioso in C (from op. 59)

appoggiaturas

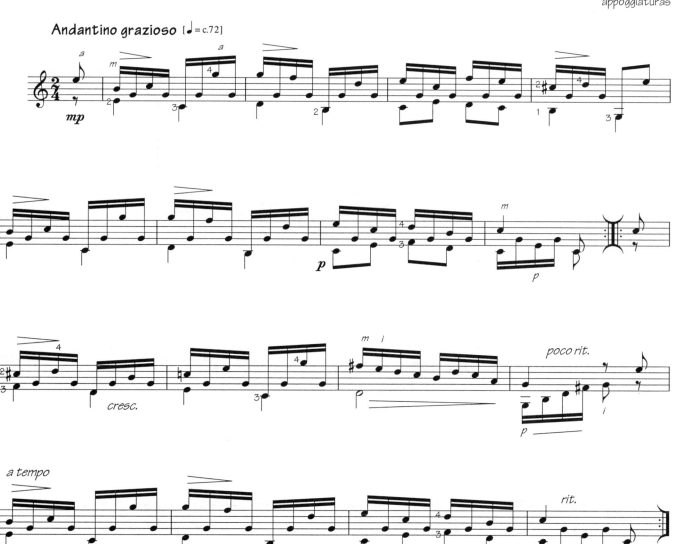

The downbeats of measures 1, 2, 4, etc., contain appoggiaturas - notes that do not harmonize with the bass and which move by step to a note that does. These expressive figures are found in many types of music and are almost always played by making a small diminuendo between the dissonant note and its resolution (as shown by the dynamic "hairpin" marks provided by Carcassi in those measures) - a sighing effect.

From *Méthode complète pour le guitare, op. 59* (Paris, c. 1840).

Matteo CARCASSI
(1792-1853)

Prelude in a-minor (from op. 59)

LH: sequential changes

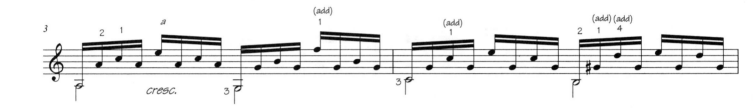

The challenges in this piece is to avoid clipping the final notes of several of the chords. Study the left-hand fingerings carefully, since they are intended to help avoid this.

From *Méthode complète pour la guitare*, op. 59 (Paris, c. 1840).

Mauro GIULIANI   [Level 2]
(1780-1829)

Allegro in a-minor (*Le papillon* - "*Butterflies*" - op. 50, no. 13)

LH: fixed finger / fast skips
RH: damping

There are several places in this piece where a finger jumps from one
string to another on successive notes (for example, measure 4). Wait until
the last possible moment, moving the finger only as the right hand plucks
the string - a bit tricky, but an important aspect of clean playing.

It is also important to observe the rests in the bass.

From *Le Papillon, op. 50* (Vienna, 1815).

Mauro GIULIANI

(1780-1829)

Andantino in C (*Le papillon - "Butterflies" - op. 50, no. 1*)

RH: p on the higher strings
LH: skips

From *Le Papillon, op. 50* (Vienna, 1815).

40

Fernando SOR (1878-1839) /
Napolean COSTE (1806-1883)

[Level 2]

Study No. 5

LH: counterpoint / fixed fingers

[Allegretto (in 2)] [♩ = c.88]

Hold the left-hand fingers down for their full written values.
Take care especially in measures 5-6 and 12-15.

From *Méthode complète pour la Guitare*, ed. Napoean Coste (Paris, c.1845).

Fernando SOR
(1778-1839)

[Level 2]

Study in C (op. 60, no. 6)

LH: optional descending slurs

[Moderato] [♩ = c.84]

Signature of Fernando Sor:

> Sor did write the slurs indicated in this piece, though it can be also be played without them. An interesting slur occurs at measure 34, where the second note of the slur sounds simultaneously with the bass note.

From *Introduction à la L'Étude de la Guitare*, op. 60 (Paris, 1831).

Ernest SHAND

(1868-1924)

Study in A-major (from op. 100)

LH: position changes with guide fingers
return damping

This piece contains a series of short position changes, all of which are connected with one of more guide fingers on the same string.

In measures 9, 21, 27 and 31, after playing with the thumb, damp the previous bass note.

From *Improved Method for Guitar, op. 100* (London, 1896).

Ernest SHAND

(1868-1924)

Study in C (from op. 100)

LH: skips / brief barre

[Andantino] [♩ = c.108]

Although the "melody" of this piece is formed by the notes that fall
on the first string, the chromatic voice-leading of the inner voice,
played by the index finger, is also interesting. Try to brin this out.

From *Improved Method for Guitar, op. 100* (London, 1896).

Antonio Jiménez MANJÓN

(1866-1919)

Study No. 22 in D

legato

[Andante] [♩ = c.63]

> More chromatic voice-leading! Try to make the melody as legato (smoothly connected) as possible. Also take care not to rush the slurs in measures 10-14.

From *La Escuela de la Guitarra* (Buenos Aires, c.1900).

45

Oh Come All Ye Faithful (Adeste fideles)

(English Hymn)

RH: chordal fingerings / alternation

Arranged by Stanley Yates

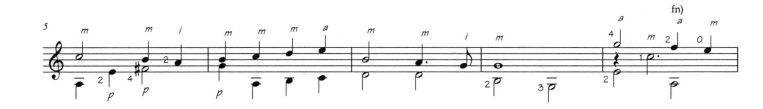

When the two-string barre is raised in measures 18-19, the first finger
should pivot neatly on to the second string. The slightly unusual fingering
in measure 9 is intended to help guarantee a legato melody.

We Three Kings

LH: l.v. overlapping fingerings

Arranged by Stanley Yates

Moderately fast (in 1) ♩. = c.63

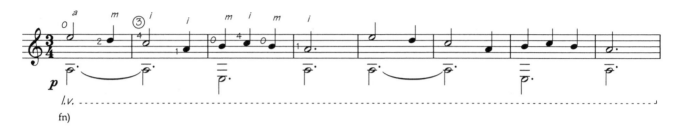

l.v. (lassicare vibrare) - "let ring." An atmospheric (slightly mysterious) harp-like effect of allowing the notes to ring over one another (regardless of melodic or harmonic considerations), created by leaving the fingers down as long as possible — might take a bit of thought.

Greensleeves (What Child Is This?)
(16th-Century English Folksong)

Arranged by Stanley Yates

This is the melody as I heard it growing up in England - some people prefer g-sharps in measures 8 and 24 (personally, I prefer the older modal-sounding g-naturals). On the topic of modes, this is a Dorian-mode melody, and the F# in measure 2 is correct!

Greensleeves is a English Renaissance tune often attributed to King Henry VIII, who did not write it - many versions of this piece exist and the precise origin is unknown.

ANON (c. 1600)
[Level 2]

2 Renaissance Dances

3-string barre

1 - The Parlement (England)

Arranged by Stanley Yates

From the Dowland Lute Book (England, c. 1600).

2 - Spagnoletta (Italy)

2 Japanese Pieces

No. 1 Koto

natural harmonics with fretted notes in high position

l.v. (*lasciare vibrare*) - let the notes ring over one another
vib. - vibrato, pull the string back and forth by rocking the left-hand

This piece emulates the sound of the *koto* - a Japanese zither-like instrument - and consists mostly of open strings with occasional fretted notes in the tenth position and harmonics in the twelfth position.

There is no time signature, nor any barlines - simply group the notes according to their relative durations.

No. 2 - Taiko

tambora

Slow dance ♩ = c.80

tambora - percussion on the bridge of the guitar with the side of right-hand thumb (sounding the strings indicated).

This piece imitates the sound of the Japanese *taiko* - a large hanging drum.

From *En mode - 22 Character Easy Pieces for Guitar.*
© 2001 Mel Bay Publications. Used with permission.

Stanley YATES

Etude mécanique No. 1

p-i-m / pi-m

Moderatey fast ♩ = c.116

cresc. poco a poco

f   sempre

cresc. poco a poco

mf   dim. e rit.   pp

> My *Etudes mécaniques* are deliberatley repetitive, though—hopefully—atmospheric.
>
> Don't be deterred by the unusual time signature, simply count in groups of threes and twos, as needed: 1-2-3, 1-2-3, 1-2, 1-2, etc.

From *Etudes mécaniques - 12 Easy-Intermediate Studies for Guitar.*

Level 3

Antonio Jiménez MANJÓN

(1866-1919)

Study No. 9 in a-minor

LH: finger 4

This piece makes full use of the left-hand little finger; be sure to position the hand fully parallel to the fingerboard, to help this finger reach the lower strings.

From *La Escuela de la Guitarra* (Buenos Aires, c.1900).

Antonio Jiménez MANJÓN
(1866-1919)

Study No. 12 in e-minor

LH: finger 4 / cross-fingering / finger exchange

Another study that makes full use of the left-hand little-finger; position the finger close to its target frets well ahead of time.

Measure 14 uses a "finger-exchange," in which the fingering changes, even though the chord remains the same, to prepare for an otherwise awkward change in measure 16.

Measure 46 uses a "cross-fingering" - fingers 1 and 2 remain in position while finger 3 temporarily plays one fret lower than usual.

From *La Escuela de la Guitarra* (Buenos Aires, c.1900).

Dionisio AGUADO
(1784-1849)

Arpeggio Study in a-minor

LH: full first position

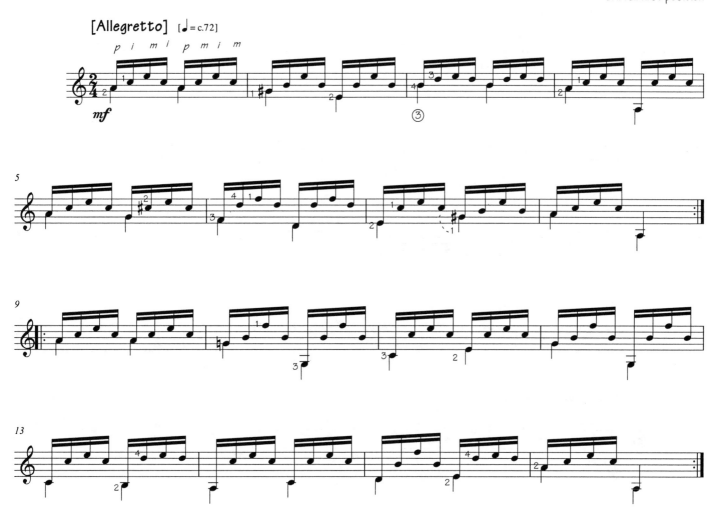

Play the notes in measure 3 as indicated (instead of with fingers 1 and 2); this will help develop left-hand position and reach (try to hold fingers 3 and 4 over their target frets ahead of playing them).

The following preparatory exercise might help (it's always possible to make up little exercise to help overcome the difficulties found in pieces):

From *Nuevo Métoda* (Madrid, 1843).

Fernando SOR (1878-1839) /
Napolean COSTE (1806-1883)

Studies 14 and 16 in C

LH: counterpoint / legato / fixed fingers

In measure 19 of the second study, use finger 2 as a "pivot" while the other fingers find their places.

Hold the left-hand fingers down for their full written values!

From *Méthode complète pour la Guitare,* ed. Napoean Coste (Paris, c.1845).

Fernando SOR

(1778-1839)

[Level 3]

Study in C (op. 60, no. 13)

LH: frequent movements

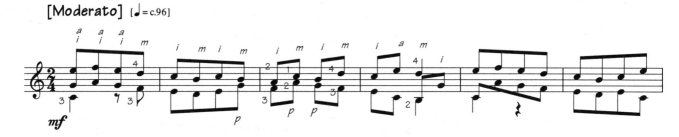

> The descending slur in measure 23 is a little tricky. Try not to clip the last note of the previous measure in preparing the first finger for this slur, and don't rush!

From *Introduction à la L'Étude de la Guitare, op. 60* (Paris, 1831).

Fernando SOR
(1778-1839)

[Level 3]

Study in a-minor (op. 60, no. 5)

RH: i-m alternation with a string crossings
LH: descending slurs

From *Introduction à la L'Étude de la Guitare, op. 60* (Paris, 1831).

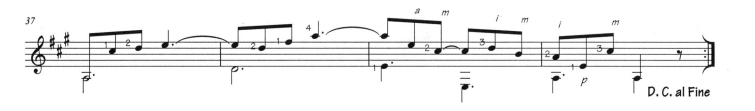

D. C. al Fine

There are two types of descending slurs in this piece: a simple type, in measures 27 and 36, where a left-hand finger "pulls-off" (plucks) an open string; and a more difficult type, in measure 4, where a left-hand finger (4) pulls-off to another fretted note - be sure to place fingers 1 and 4 together. There is also a tendency to rush slurs, so take care to play in time.

Also take care to damp any potentially over-ringing open bass-notes, as discussed earlier.

Drawing from Sor's *Guitar Method* (London, 1832), showing the typical playing position used by French and Italian guitarists of the time (to which Sor objected).

Fernando SOR
(1778-1839)

Andantino (op. 44, no. 9)

LH: more extended shapes / second position /
legato voice-leading

(Choral)

The main goal with this piece is to have completely smooth connections
between the notes of each of the three "voice" parts.

As always, think carefully about using hand-positions that will place the
fingers where they need to be (whether parallel to the fingerboard or rotated
to some degree), and try to position free fingers as close as possible to their
target frets ready for the next chord shape.

From *Vingt-quatre Petites Pièces Progressives, op.44* (Paris, 1831).

Antonio NAVA

(1775-1828)

Andante in A

LH: second-position /
guide-finger position changes
RH: damping

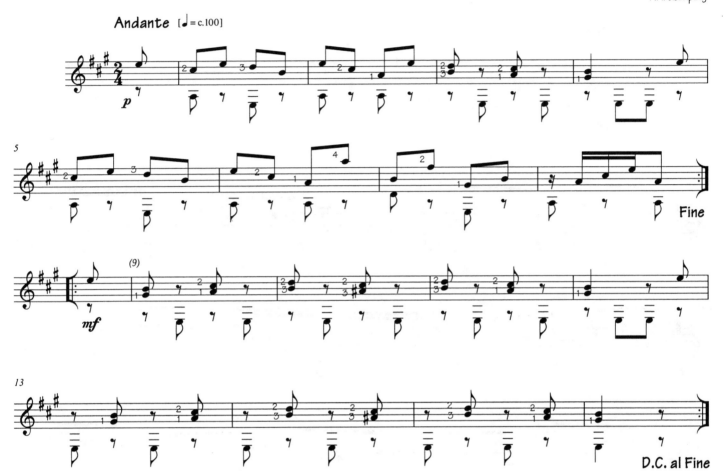

The essential ingredient of this amusing study lies the articulation of the bass-part, where the notes need to be damped with the thumb.

Signature of Antonio Nava:

Antonio Nava

From *Metodo per Chitarra* (Milan, 1812).

Ferdinando CARULLI
(1770-1841)

Waltz in D (op. 121, no.3)

LH: second position

When playing in the full second position (with finger 4 playing at the fifth
fret), be sure to use a "parallel" hand position - the palm of the hand parallel
to the edge of the fingerboard, with all fingers lined-up along the first string.
Try measures 2, 15 and 17 to get the idea.

From *Vingt-Quatre Pièces pour Guitarre op. 121* (Paris, c. 1815).

Ferdinando CARULLI
(1770-1841)

Andantino in a-minor (op. 241, no.19)

optional ascending and descending slurs /
finger 4

In places such as measure 9, it's easier to move the entire hand rather than reach for the notes (with the weaker fourth finger).

From *Methode complète pour pincer le guitare, op. 241* (Paris, c. 1825).

Matteo CARCASSI
(1778-1839)

Minuet and Trio (op. 21, no. 12)

chordal fingerings / short scales

MINUET

From *Vingt-quatre petite pièces pour le guitar, op. 21* (Paris, c. 1835).

Minuet (variation)

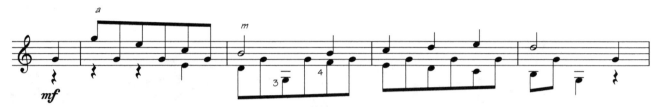

The short scales in the Trio are fairly quick and are best practiced separately.

Be sure to play the indicated dynamics throughout.

Johann Kaspar MERTZ
(1806-1856)

[Level 3]

Romance

legato /
distant position-changes
(prepared by open strings)

Adagio [♩ = c.76]

Adagio means "very slow"!

Measure 4: be sure to switch between parallel and rotated hand positions.

Measure 10: use the open string to give you the time to make the shift;
finger 3 should be "shaped" and in position for the high B before you
actually fret the note. It's also possible to simplify this measure, as follows:

Ossia:

Measure 11: work on the rhythm first, counting without the guitar.

Measures 16-18: same general advise for the position shifts as given for measure 10.

This is a beautiful piece, and well worth a little effort!

From *Schule für die Guitare* (Vienna, c. 1847).

Anon-Traditional

The Banks of Newfoundland
(19th-Century Sea Shanty)

RH: damping and articulation with the thumb /
rolled chords

Arranged by Roger Hudson

> You ramblin' boys of Liverpool,
> I'll have you beware,
> When you go in a Yankee packet ship...
>
> Be sure to damp the basses throughout and to articulate
> the short basses in measures 8-9, 16-7 and 24-5.

short appoggiaturas (quick ascending slurs)

Amazing Grace

Arranged by Stanley Yates

Moderately slow [♩=c.112]

The second strain of this arrangement (measures 17-32) uses some short *appgoggiatura*s - play the small note on the beat, with the rest of the chord, then slur onto the main note.

The Coventry Carol

free-finger position changes

Arranged by Stanley Yates

This piece is has been arranged in Renaissance lute style. Lutenists often based their solo pieces on well-known songs of the time, adding their own variations to the melody in the form of "divisions" — dividing the original melody notes into more notes of shorter value (as in the second strain of this arrangement).

Guillaume MORLAYE
(c. 1515-c. 1565)

3 Dances from Renaissance France

1 - BRANLE (1)

Arranged by Stanley Yates

2 - ALLEMANDE

3 - BRANLE (2)

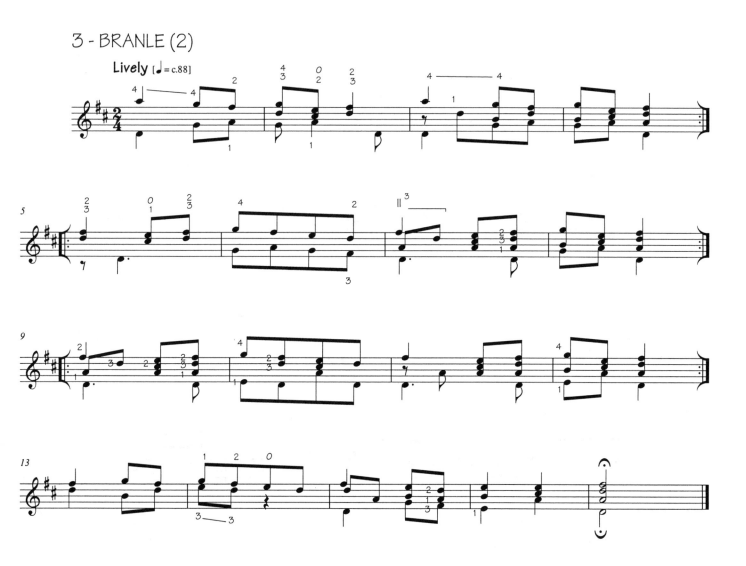

The guitar (with only four strings) was a very popular instrument in France during the mid-sixteenth century. Guitar music at that time was written in tablature (see below), much like modern guitar tablature. The three pieces transcribed here are, believe it or not, just about the least difficult pieces for guitar that I could find from that time!

Orginal tablature of the Branle transcribed above:

Title page of Morlaye's *First Book* of guitar music (Paris, 1552):

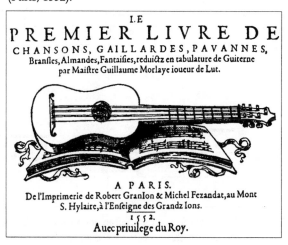

From *Le Premier Livre ... de Guiterne* (Paris, 1552).

73

Lucas de RIBAYEZ
(fl. c. 1680-1700)

[Level 3]

2 Dances from Baroque Spain

second position / optional trills

Arranged by Stanley Yates

The *gaita* is a lively folk dance, often accompanied by bagpipes. "La batalla" is a reference to battle-music, which was often used as the basis of instrumental compositions in Baroque Spain — the style is based on the bugle-calls (*clarines*) used in battle.

From *Luz y norte musicale...por...la guitarra* (Madrid, 1677).

Jean Phillippe RAMEAU
(1683-1764)

[Level 3]

Le Tambourine

2 and 3-note slurs / positions I and V

Arranged by Stanley Yates

This is arrangement is based on a well-known harpsichord piece by Rameau, and has makes a good slur study. Most of these slurs should be practiced separately, paying attention to hand position and rhythm.

From *Pièces pour Clavecin* (Paris, 1724).

Stanley YATES

3 Baroque Dances (from "Short Suite in Baroque Style")

3 - SARABANDA

4 - GAVOTTA

5 - GIGA

Lively ♩. = c.116

Kean O'Hara (Irish Harp Piece, c. 1700)

optional light slurs

Arranged by Stanley Yates

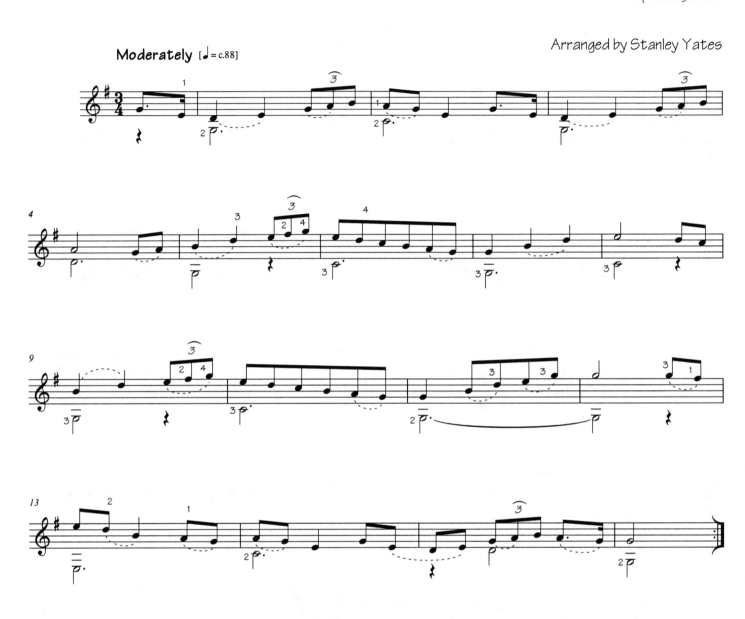

This evocative piece can be played with or without the indicated slurs, or with some but not all. The more slurring used, the more you will need to practice! On the other hand, light, even slurring, with good rhythm, brings a singing quality to the guitar that cannot be emulated by plucking alone. So, do whatever you need to make the piece sound good!

From *A Favourite Collection of Old Irish Tunes* (Dublin, c. 1780).

Carlo DOMENICONI   [Level 3]

Klangbilder ("Soundfigures")
- No. 20 from *24 Klangbilder*

alternation / LH independence

Be sure to observe the articulation indications in measures 4 and 15,
and to hold the longer notes for their full written value.

Klangbilder ("Soundfigures")
- No. 24 from *24 Klangbilder*

Try to balance the accompaniment and the melody, perhaps using a different tone for each.

Andrew YORK

Chant (from *8 Discernments*)

counterpoint / legato

When practicing this piece take time to listen to the longer notes as the more active ones move around them. Get to know the two individual parts by practicing them separately.

8 Discernments for Guitar. Copyright © 1994 Seven Centers Publishing (BMI). Worldwide print rights assigned to Guitar Solo Publications (ASCAP). Used by permission.

Nikita KOSHKIN

Clair de Lune ("Reflections of the Moon")

(No. 12 from 24 Mascarades)

natural harmonics

Mascarades for Guitar. © 1987 Editions Henry Lemoine.
41 rue Bayen 75017 Paris. Used with Permission.

Mode Bulgaro

7/8 meter / sudden character contrasts

Count the rhythm as follows: 1-2, 1-2, 1-2-3, until comfortable.

From *En Mode - 22 Easy Pieces for Guitar*.

Stanley YATES

Etude mécanique No. 3

p-i-m / 2-1 descending slur /
dynamics

This piece has a decided Eastern flavor to it. Or is it Spanish? (Don't ask me).
Be sure to observe the written dynamics, and remember that a simple
descending slur is the equivalent of a left-hand finger plucking the string
instead a right-hand one.

can also be played:

Rainy Scene

syncopation / ascending slurs

If you have trouble working out the syncopated rhythms in this piece, count-
out the composite rhythm the parts make together. For example, measure 1
would be 1 & 2 & 3 & ; measures 17-18 would be 1 2 & 3 / 1 & 2 & 3.

An Old Story (no. 1 from *15 Descriptive Pieces*)

changing meters / accentuation

> A modern take on Renaissance music, this piece uses frequent meter
> changes. Practice counting the beats (1-2-3, 1-2-3, 1-2, 1-2, 1-2, 1-2-3, etc.) ,
> without the guitar, until this feels comfortable.

Stepan RAK

[Level 3]

Country Dance (no. 8 from *15 Descriptive Pieces*)

double-notes with the thumb / accentution

Again, practice counting the rhythm away from the guitar.

Ragtime (no. 17 from *20 Jazz-Images*)

Short Blues

Music in this style is usually written in "equal" eighth-notes, but is meant
to be played in "swing" eight-notes - like the first and third notes of a triplet.
The rhythms in measures 8 and 17 almost certainly will need to be practiced
without the guitar - don't guess!

From *En Mode - 22 Easy Character Pieces for Guitar.*
© 2001 Mel Bay Publications. Used with permission.

New Didactic Works by Stanley Yates

En Mode - 22 Easy Character Pieces for Guitar

1 - Prelude

2 - Valse Russe

3 - Folksong

4 - Old Dance

5 - Musette

6 - Koto

7 - Taiko

8 - Jasmine

9 - Prelude

10 - Allemande

11 - Sarabande

12 - Gavotta

13 - Giga

14 - Villanella

15 - Tango antigua

16 - Polka

17 - Malaguenesque

18 - Processional

19 - Mode Bulgaro

20 - Amazonia

21 - Tango nuevo

22 - Short Blues

No. 1

No. 2

No. 3

No. 4

No. 5

No. 6

No. 7

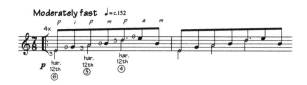

No. 8

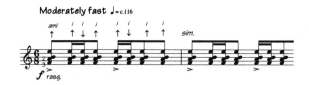

No. 9

No. 10

No. 11

No. 12